Documents of American Democracy

U.S. CONSTITUTION

Kristen Rajczak Nelson

New York

Published in 2017 by The Rosen Publishing Group, Inc.
29 East 21st Street, New York, NY 10010

Editor: Katie Kawa
Book Design: Tanya Dellaccio

Photo Credits: Cover (painting) https://commons.wikimedia.org/wiki/File:Scene_at_the_Signing_of_the_Constitution_of_the_United_States.jpg; cover, p. 13 (document) https://commons.wikimedia.org/wiki/File:Constitution_of_the_United_States,_page_1.jpg; background (all pages except 13) Didecs/Shutterstock.com; pp. 5,9 Hulton Archive/Getty Images; p. 7 (bottom) DeAgostini/Getty Images; p. 7 (Ben Franklin) https://commons.wikimedia.org/wiki/File:BenFranklinDuplessis.jpg; p. 7 (George Washington) https://en.wikipedia.org/wiki/File:Gilbert_Stuart_Williamstown_Portrait_of_George_Washington.jpg; p. 11 Courtesy of the National Archives; p. 13 Everett Historical/Shutterstock.com; p. 15 (John Adams) https://commons.wikimedia.org/wiki/File:Official_Presidential_potrait_of_John_Adams_(by_John_Trumbull,_circa_1792).jpg; p. 15 (Frederick Muhlenberg) https://commons.wikimedia.org/wiki/File:Frederick_Muhlenberg.jpg; p. 17 MPI/Getty Images; p. 19 Joseph Sohm/Shutterstock.com; p. 21 (Washington) Archive Photos/Getty Images; p. 21 (Obama) https://commons.wikimedia.org/wiki/File:US_President_Barack_Obama_taking_his_Oath_of_Office_-_2009Jan20.jpg; p. 23 (White House) vichie81/Shutterstock.com; p. 23 (Capitol) Mikhail Kolesnikov/Shutterstock.com; p. 23 (Supreme Court Building) Matt Snodderly/Shutterstock.com; p. 25 KAREN BLEIER/Getty Images; p. 27 (George Mason) https://commons.wikimedia.org/wiki/File:George_Mason_portrait.jpg; p. 27 (Patrick Henry) https://commons.wikimedia.org/wiki/File:Patrick_henry.JPG; p. 27 (The Federalist) https://commons.wikimedia.org/wiki/File:The_Federalist_(1st_ed,_1788,_vol_I,_title_page)_-_02.jpg; p. 29 (Bill of Rights) https://commons.wikimedia.org/wiki/File:Bill_of_Rights_Pg1of1_AC.jpg; p. 29 (James Madison) https://commons.wikimedia.org/wiki/File:James_Madison.jpg.

Library of Congress Cataloging-in-Publication Data

Names: Rajczak Nelson, Kristen, author.
Title: U.S. Constitution / Kristen Rajczak Nelson.
Other titles: United States Constitution
Description: New York : PowerKids Press, 2017. | Series: Documents of
  American democracy | Includes index.
Identifiers: LCCN 2016011887 | ISBN 9781499420890 (pbk.) | ISBN 9781499420913 (library bound) | ISBN 9781499420906 (6 pack)
Subjects: LCSH: Constitutional history–United States–Juvenile literature. |
  Constitutional law–United States–Juvenile literature. | United States.
  Constitution–Juvenile literature.
Classification: LCC KF4541 .R348 2017 | DDC 342.7302–dc23
LC record available at http://lccn.loc.gov/2016011887

Manufactured in the United States of America

CPSIA Compliance Information: Batch #BS16PK: For Further Information contact Rosen Publishing, New York, New York at 1-800-237-9932

CONTENTS

THE LAW OF THE LAND

The "supreme law" of the United States is the U.S. Constitution. After the American Revolution, many Americans feared a strong central government. They'd just won a war against a powerful government and worked to make sure the new U.S. government didn't have too much power. However, after one failed constitution that gave little power to a central government, it was clear that thinking needed to change.

The framers of the U.S. Constitution worked to establish a government that didn't favor large or small states. They balanced the central government's power by creating three branches: executive, judicial, and legislative. In addition, they learned from the past and promised citizens protection from both outside forces and excessive government control. When completed, the U.S. Constitution created our nation's government as we know it today, and it continues to be the foundation for American democracy.

THE ARTICLES OF CONFEDERATION

*Following the American Revolution, the United States created its first constitution. The Articles of Confederation went into effect in 1781. At the time, most Americans felt more loyalty to their state than to the new federal government. Because of this, the document gave states a lot of independence. However, the weak central government couldn't raise money for itself, and it couldn't effectively respond to **crises** such as uprisings. By 1787, many were calling to improve the document.*

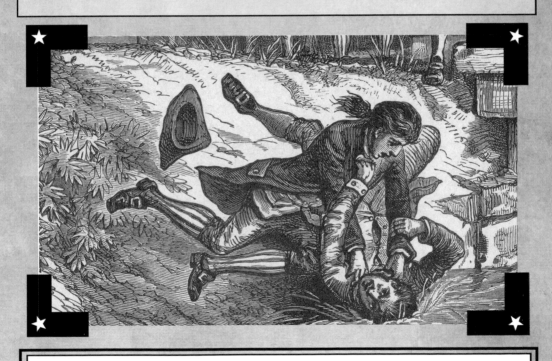

*The Articles of Confederation mainly **allied** the states so they could protect themselves if the need arose. However, when an uprising called Shays's Rebellion, shown here, happened within the United States, the young federal government couldn't do much about it. The lack of a strong central response to that uprising helped many see that the Articles of Confederation needed changes.*

THE CONSTITUTIONAL CONVENTION

Delegates from 12 states gathered in May 1787 in Philadelphia, Pennsylvania, to begin reforming the Articles of Confederation. Rhode Island didn't send any delegates. The states' representatives were scholars, politicians, and men who'd been leaders during the war. Benjamin Franklin, who was 81 at the time, was the oldest delegate present. George Washington was named president of what's become known as the Constitutional Convention.

The delegates realized early on they would need to write a document that would replace the Articles of Confederation altogether. All debates that occurred during the convention were kept secret so every man there would speak his mind—and there were many debates! A stronger central government that included citizen representation was surely needed, but many states' representatives didn't agree on how that should be done.

BENJAMIN FRANKLIN

GEORGE WASHINGTON

The Constitutional Convention lasted until September 1787.

The first major compromise of the Constitutional Convention had to do with how states would be represented in Congress. The Virginia Plan called for representation to be based on a state's population, which favored larger states. The New Jersey Plan proposed that all states should have the same number of representatives. This would help states with smaller populations have a voice in the federal government. The Great Compromise, or Connecticut Compromise, **merged** these two plans to create the two-house Congress included in the Constitution. A state's number of representatives in the House of Representatives is based on population, while all states have two seats in the Senate.

THE SLAVERY ISSUE

At the time of the Constitutional Convention, slavery was still a big part of the southern economy. The delegates from the southern states were very protective of their right to own slaves, making it a challenge to include anything about slavery in the U.S. Constitution. Some delegates from the North wanted to outlaw slavery or, at the very least, end the slave trade. In the end, though, they chose to keep the peace at the Constitutional Convention rather than push for such a change.

The Three-Fifths Compromise arose following the Great Compromise. It answered the question of how slaves would be counted toward a state's population when considering representation. For every five slaves, three would be counted.

The word "slave" doesn't appear in the U.S. Constitution. However, certain rights of slave owners were protected. The Constitution made it law that a "person held to Service or Labour" must be returned to the person "to whom such Service or Labour may be due."

"No Person held to Service or Labour in one State, under the Laws thereof, escaping into another, shall, in Consequence of any Law or Regulation therein, be discharged from such Service or Labour, but shall be delivered up on Claim of the Party to whom such Service or Labour may be due."

WRITING AND SIGNING

The first **draft** of the U.S. Constitution was delivered to the members of the convention on August 6, 1787. The convention debated it for about a month before five men were chosen as the Committee of Style: Alexander Hamilton of New York, William Samuel Johnson of Connecticut, Gouverneur Morris of Pennsylvania, James Madison of Virginia, and Rufus King of Massachusetts. They presented an edited document on September 12.

Of the 55 delegates who attended the Constitutional Convention, 39 signed the completed U.S. Constitution. Some had left earlier in the summer. A few didn't want to sign it, including at least one delegate who believed it should have outlawed slavery. The document the 39 delegates signed on September 17, 1787, is the oldest written constitution still in use today!

> *The original U.S. Constitution can be seen today at the National Archives in Washington, D.C.*

Each part of the
Constitution
is called an
article.

Each article
is numbered
using Roman
numerals.

The first draft of the
Constitution had 23
articles. There are
seven today.

The 39 signatures on
the Constitution are
grouped by state.

The date the
Constitution was
signed is written out
in words.

The preamble of the U.S. Constitution is only 52 words long, but they're packed with meaning:

"We the People of the United States, in Order to form a more perfect Union, establish Justice, insure domestic Tranquility, provide for the common defence, promote the general Welfare, and secure the Blessings of Liberty to ourselves and our Posterity, do ordain and establish this Constitution for the United States of America."

A preamble is an introduction to a document, and it often tells the reasons the document was written. The Constitution's preamble does exactly that. It states that the people of the United States want to establish the laws of their nation, including those needed to maintain peace within the country, protect the country, and ensure citizens live happy and free lives in the present and in the future.

THE AUTHOR

*Gouverneur Morris was quite influential in the writing of the Constitution. The preamble in particular bears his mark. He fought for the introductory phrase "We the People" as opposed to the list of states an earlier draft included. James Madison later argued in favor of including Morris's phrase, saying, "It will be then a government established by the 13 states of America, not through the **intervention** of the legislatures, but by the people at large."*

GOUVERNEUR MORRIS

The preamble of the U.S. Constitution, shown here, is often quoted because it seems to capture the spirit of the founding of the United States—the creation of "a more perfect Union" through representation by the people.

ARTICLE I: CONGRESS

The U.S. Constitution is divided into seven articles. Article I is the longest. It states that Congress, which is made up of the Senate and the House of Representatives, is given the legislative powers of the nation.

Article I first introduces the House of Representatives, stating representatives will serve terms lasting two years. Then, it gives two main qualifications for those chosen to serve in the House. A representative must be at least 25 years old and have been a U.S. citizen for at least seven years. The section further states that population will determine the number of representatives for each state.

The Senate is similarly presented. Each state has two senators that serve six-year terms. A senator must be at least 30 years old and have been a U.S. citizen for at least nine years.

> *According to Article I of the Constitution, the Speaker of the House leads the House of Representatives. The vice president, who only votes when there's a tie in the Senate, is the head of the Senate.*

FREDERICK AUGUSTUS CONRAD MUHLENBERG
FIRST SPEAKER OF THE HOUSE

"All legislative Powers herein granted shall be vested in a Congress of the United States, which shall consist of a Senate and House of Representatives."

JOHN ADAMS
FIRST VICE PRESIDENT

Article I includes instructions on how Congress should conduct its business, including that it should meet at least once a year. It also states how representatives and senators should be paid and requires that members of the House and Senate take notes of each meeting for the public to see. It further states how bills proposed in Congress become laws. Bills for "raising Revenue," such as taxes, are only allowed to start in the House. Other bills can come from either the House or Senate and must be approved by both before they move on to the president.

Congress's other duties and powers are also listed in Article I. Collecting taxes, overseeing international trade, creating a postal service, and declaring war are just some of them. Congress's final job listed in the U.S. Constitution is to make any laws needed to carry out the powers stated in the Constitution.

The Constitution clearly states powers Congress doesn't have, too. For example, it can't grant a noble title to anyone. It also can't show favoritism to one state or area over another.

VETO POWER

The U.S. government is based on a system of checks and balances. The president is able to "check" Congress by using the presidential power to veto, or stop, any law Congress passes. If this happens, the bill can be reworked according to the president's objections by the house it started in. If both houses pass the reworked bill with a two-thirds majority, the bill becomes a law. A bill can also become a law if the president doesn't sign it or veto it within 10 days of receiving it.

The second article of the U.S. Constitution gives the president the "executive Power" of the country. This means the president's main job is to oversee the running of the United States. Article II outlines how the president is elected.

Each state chooses a group of people called electors who are part of what's now called the Electoral College. The number of electors is equal to how many senators and representatives the state has in Congress. Each elector casts one vote for a presidential candidate who can be from their state and one vote for a candidate who must not be from their

★ ★ ★ ★ ★ ★ ★ ★ ★ ★ ★ ★ ★ ★ ★ ★ ★

MORE ABOUT THE ELECTORAL COLLEGE

Many people find the Electoral College system confusing and unnecessary. In almost all states, every electoral vote goes to the candidate who wins the majority of the popular vote in that state. It's rare that an elector doesn't vote for whom they're supposed to. Even though some argue that the presidential election process should change, there's only been one change to the system since the Constitution was written. In 1804, the Constitution was changed so candidates run for either president or vice president and the electors vote for them separately.

18

The Constitution states that the president must be a "natural
born Citizen, or a Citizen of the United States," be at least 35
years old, and have lived in the country for at least 14 years. This
document sets the term length for the president at four years.

state. Although it's not stated in the Constitution, it's common
practice for electors to vote based on the **popular vote** in
their state. According to the Constitution as it was written in
1787, the person who wins the majority becomes president
and the runner-up becomes vice president.

The powers of the president are outlined in Article II of the Constitution, too. The president is named the commander in chief of all the armed forces of the United States and has the ability to pardon people who've committed crimes against the United States.

The president has the power to make treaties and appoint **ambassadors**, Supreme Court justices, and other major officers who haven't been named in the Constitution. In the spirit of checks and balances, though, these treaties and appointments have to be approved by the Senate. The Constitution also gives the president the power to **convene** Congress in times of emergency.

Both Article I and Article II explain how the president can be removed from office by the power of Congress, should he or she break the law. This process is called impeachment.

★ ★ ★ ★ ★ ★ ★ ★ ★ ★ ★ ★ ★ ★ ★ ★

THE VICE PRESIDENT

*Article II also outlines the job of the vice president—but it's not much to go on. It does state that if the president should die, resign, or otherwise become unable to do the job, the powers of the office "**devolve**" on the vice president. When President William Henry Harrison died in 1841, Vice President John Tyler took this to mean that the vice president became president. No one challenged him, so he became president! This path of **succession** was officially made law in the 25th Amendment, or change, to the Constitution.*

On the day the president is inaugurated, or formally admitted to public office, they take what's called an oath of office. The words of this oath come from Article II of the U.S. Constitution.

GEORGE WASHINGTON'S INAUGURATION

BARACK OBAMA'S INAUGURATION

"Before he enter on the Execution of his Office, he shall take the following Oath or Affirmation:—'I do solemnly swear (or affirm) that I will faithfully execute the Office of President of the United States, and will to the best of my Ability, preserve, protect and defend the Constitution of the United States.'"

ARTICLE III: THE SUPREME COURT

The third article of the U.S. Constitution establishes a judicial system, but it only gives specific instructions about the highest court in the nation, which we call the Supreme Court. This court only handles certain kinds of cases, according to the Constitution. These cases include those between one state and another, those between citizens and states, and those involving ambassadors or **maritime** law.

The Supreme Court mainly hears cases concerning the Constitution. The decisions made by Supreme Court justices have played a big part in the interpretation of the Constitution over time, making its meaning clearer and applying it to modern situations.

While the president appoints Supreme Court justices, they have to be approved by the Senate. The power to create the lower court system is also given to Congress.

> *The Constitution sets up the three branches of U.S. government. Each branch is kept from having too much power through a system of checks and balances.*

The Three Branches of U.S. Government

EXECUTIVE	LEGISLATIVE	JUDICIAL
headed by the president	*Congress*	*Supreme Court is highest U.S. court*
makes sure laws are carried out	*makes laws*	*includes all other lower courts*
has veto power over Congress	*has power of impeachment of president and other government officials*	*interprets Constitution*
appoints Supreme Court justices	*approves Supreme Court justice appointments*	*makes sure the rights guaranteed in the Constitution are upheld*

THE WHITE HOUSE   **THE CAPITOL**   **THE SUPREME COURT BUILDING**

With the three major branches of government outlined, the Constitution then focuses on the states. Article IV requires the states to respect the laws of other states and allows for the addition of future states. It also gives every U.S. state a guarantee of protection and proper representation in the government.

Article V describes two ways the Constitution can be amended, but only the first has been used. Two-thirds of both the House of Representatives and the Senate must pass the proposed amendment. Then, three-fourths of the states need to **ratify** the amendment.

Article VI makes the Constitution the highest law of the United States. It also declares that all elected officials will promise to uphold it.

In Article IV, the U.S. government promises the states it will protect them. The Constitution empowers Congress to raise a navy and other armed forces to aid in keeping this promise.

"The United States shall guarantee to every State in this Union a Republican Form of Government, and shall protect each of them against Invasion; and on Application of the Legislature, or of the Executive (when the Legislature cannot be convened), against domestic Violence."

RATIFICATION

The final article of the Constitution explains the process for its ratification. Nine of the 13 states had to approve it.

Following the Constitutional Convention, the state leaders who had to vote on the document's approval generally divided into two groups. The Federalists supported the Constitution, and the Anti-Federalists didn't. One major issue the Anti-Federalists had was that the Constitution didn't directly address basic civil rights of citizens. This caused great debate in many states, including North Carolina. In fact, North Carolina refused to ratify the document until it was promised that the Constitution would be amended to clearly protect citizens' rights.

On December 7, 1787, Delaware became the first state to ratify the Constitution. When New Hampshire became the ninth state to ratify it, the date was set for the Constitution to go into effect: March 9, 1789.

Some of the most outspoken Anti-Federalists were George Mason and Patrick Henry, shown here. The protection of individual rights was very important to the Anti-Federalists.

THE FEDERALIST PAPERS

One way the Federalists gathered support for the Constitution was through 85 essays now commonly called the Federalist Papers. Written by James Madison, Alexander Hamilton, and John Jay, the articles explained the content and layout of the Constitution to the people it would govern. The Federalist Papers were published in Independent Journal *and* New York Packet *between October 1787 and August 1788. These essays give great insight into how the Founding Fathers— at least the Federalists—interpreted the Constitution.*

GEORGE MASON

PATRICK HENRY

THE BILL OF RIGHTS

When Congress first met in 1789, James Madison presented possible amendments to the Constitution proposed by the states. Ten of these were ratified and make up one of the most important parts of the Constitution for U.S. citizens: the Bill of Rights. These amendments are a list of the civil rights guaranteed under the highest law of the land, the Constitution. This is what the Anti-Federalists wanted.

Among the amendments included in the Bill of Rights, the First Amendment guarantees freedom of religion, speech, the press, and assembly, as well as the right to ask the government to fix problems. The Fifth Amendment gives citizens the right to due process, which means fair judicial treatment. The Ninth Amendment states that civil rights not listed in the Constitution will also be upheld. The 10th Amendment gives all powers not assigned to the federal government to the states.

The Bill of Rights was adopted in 1791. The original copy of the document, shown here, has faded over time.

THE AMENDMENTS

The Constitution has been amended 27 times since it was ratified. Three amendments were adopted in response to the American Civil War. The 13th Amendment outlaws slavery in the United States, the 14th Amendment guarantees all citizens equal protection under the law, and the 15th Amendment states all male citizens have the right to vote—no matter their race. Other famous amendments include the 19th Amendment, which grants women the right to vote, and the 22nd Amendment, which limits the number of presidential terms to two.

JAMES MADISON

INTERPRETING THE CONSTITUTION

The U.S. Constitution is interpreted every day by the president, Congress, and the Supreme Court, as well as courts and lawmakers at the state and local levels. Some interpretations of the Constitution have become law through decisions made on cases brought before the Supreme Court. The Bill of Rights in particular has needed interpretation, such as explaining the limits of free speech and the right to bear arms. These decisions have a direct effect on U.S. citizens' lives. Even young people have been affected by Supreme Court decisions to stop school **segregation** and define freedom of the press in schools.

The U.S. Constitution is a living document that still has the possibility for change. It shaped a nation, but the nation continues to shape it as well.

GLOSSARY

ally: To join together for a common purpose.

ambassador: An official representative or messenger, especially to another country.

convene: To come together to meet.

crisis: An unstable or difficult situation.

delegate: A person sent to a meeting or convention to represent others.

devolve: To pass from one person to another at a lower level of authority.

draft: A piece of writing.

intervention: The act of taking action about something to affect the outcome.

maritime: Having to do with trade on the sea.

merge: To combine.

popular vote: The votes of the general population of a place.

ratify: To formally approve.

segregation: The separation of people based on race, class, or ethnicity.

succession: The order in which something happens.

INDEX

WEBSITES

Due to the changing nature of Internet links, PowerKids Press has
developed an online list of websites related to the subject of this book.
This site is updated regularly. Please use this link to access the list:
www.powerkidslinks.com/amdoc/con